ISBN 978-1-312-86355-2

The
WEALTHY Mindset
77 Wealth Secrets To Make You
Richer In All Areas Of Your Life

Disclaimer

This e-book has been written for information purposes only. Every effort has been made to make this ebook as complete and accurate as possible. However, there may be mistakes in typography or content. Also, this e-book provides information only up to the publishing date. Therefore, this ebook should be used as a guide - not as the ultimate source.

The purpose of this ebook is to educate. The author and the publisher does not warrant that the information contained in this e-book is fully complete and shall not be responsible for any errors or omissions. The author and publisher shall have neither liability nor responsibility to any person or entity with respect to any loss or damage caused or alleged to be caused directly or indirectly by this e-book.

Table of Contents

Introduction

Being wealthy does not have to be difficult if you have the know-how. In these hard economic times many people are satisfied by just getting by and scraping enough money together to pay the bills.

Wealth and financial freedom are a far-off dream for many people. For them, it means mansions, gated communities, a fast car, private parties or a pool. The truly wealthy have family names like Rockefeller or Morgan.

It can be easy to accumulate wealth. The thing is, not everyone knows how. The twentieth century has bought a boom of first-time millionaires, many of which do not come from family money. They make their first million by employing timeless wealth wisdom and secrets only the ultra rich used to know. Fortunately for you, there are dozens, even hundreds of little wealth nuggets you can easily apply to your life to expand your portfolio and double, even triple your net worth.

Being smart with money and becoming wealthy is not rocket science, but for many it looks and feels like hard work. The funny thing is it, the fact of its very simplicity means that more and more people should know and be doing this. But they are not. This is because most people do not know how to make money work for them, not the other way around. This is also because making money involves patience and restraint. Everything about our culture advocates otherwise.

But do you want to end up broke by the time you retire? Do you constantly fend off phone calls from creditors? Do you sigh and shake your head at your bank balance? No one wants to spend their life waiting for payday and watching money flutter away the moment bills come in the mail.

Becoming wealthy is not just about falling into family money, inheriting a trust fund or even having a big income. In fact, many people with huge incomes rarely are truly wealthy. Huge incomes often equal huge expenses and struggling to keep your finances in the black every month does not equal financial freedom. Investing is different from spending. Someone who has a huge house or houses and a great car may look rich but may not be.

Affluence and wealth can be hard to come by. If you are looking for secrets to getting millions or simply looking for a way to manage your money, this is it. This book will teach you the secrets of the truly wealthy and is a step-by-step guide on how to get there. You will learn everything from gaining financial freedom to basic investing and secret tips from business giants all over the world.

True financial freedom is only a step away, if you know how. Are you ready to start becoming truly wealthy? These 77 gems and secrets are designed to help you turn your resources, whatever they may be, into true wealth. This eBook can help you whether you follow it step by step or choose a few tactics to start with.

Creating a Wealth Foundation: Earning Financial Freedom

Creating the Wealth Mindset

The wealthy think differently. This is true and an inescapable fact. The other thing is that there is a poor mindset and a wealthy one.

The rich have a different approach to life. They plan, risk and manage their money in a different manner. They also have a positive attitude towards life and opportunities. The first and most important step to true financial freedom is creating this mindset for yourself. This also involves a no-holds barred, honest look at your life and assets.

Creating a starting place is as important as moving forward, so it does not matter if you start with $1 or $1,000,000. It is all about the mindset and the will to move forward to creating your wealth.

1 Redefine what wealth means for you. Being "rich" simply is a term for many people. Technically, wealth or being wealthy is defined as having an abundance of resources or possessions. The high life does not equal wealth. Having a gigantic mortgage for a beautiful home or a huge car payment does not equal wealth.

Are status symbols your end goal? Does wealth for you mean that ability not to worry about bills or how much is left in your checking account at the end of the month? Does it mean providing comfortably for your family or being free from financial worry? Does it mean the ability to afford luxury designer goods or getting a membership to the local country club? Being rich or being wealthy can also mean you enjoy a comfortable retirement.

Does wealth mean something totally different to you? Your definition of wealth goes a long way towards setting your goals.

2 Another important step when it comes to managing your wealth is to set goals. Start with an overall battle plan, such as "By the end of the year, I will have more at least $500,000 in savings." Why? You need to be a visionary to be wealthy. A common factor that sets the millionaire apart from the average Joe is this: they know they wanted to be wealthy and they were willing to take the steps to reach their goal.

To reach one goal, you have to make smaller goals and reach them. Every little step you take, every penny you save matters. Use smaller goals as stepping stones. For example, to save that $500,000, one needs to set aside $5000 every single month, invest or cut down expenses.

3 Manifest your financial destiny by setting your subconscious towards specific goals. Create dream charts by cutting out pictures of your dream status or words that empower to help fuel your subconscious and get you

to wear you want to go. Never underestimate the power of your will and mind. Wealthy people never say they cannot do it, they think of ways so that they can.

Write it down. Seeing what you want, and getting what you want involve seeing it in black and white.

4 Know how much you are worth. Take stock of all your assets and income and subtract your debt. Many people go through life financially blind, not knowing how much they are worth or how much they owe and often end up blindsided by money.

5 The test: Your age x (your average household income from all sources – inheritance) divided by 10 = your net worth. The rich have a net worth often double or triple the amount. The average American has less than half. The goal is to double your net worth.

6 The truly wealthy consider themselves as the foremost asset. Accordingly, they pay themselves first. They also tend to invest in themselves first, especially when it comes to education. Take classes and groom yourself to be the millionaire, entrepreneur and success you want to be.

7 Guard your ideas with the passion of the Secret Service. Commodities are now no longer limited to labor, but have expanded to include ideas, imagination and opportunities.

8 Keep in mind that the average millionaire is not who you think he is. The frugal rich stay richer—if you do not believe this, think of all those high flying celebrities who end up with their homes in foreclosure or selling their tell-alls on TV to pay for all that Cristal and all those houses.

The famous IKEA owner drives a Volvo. HSBC's chairperson famously goes around the main office turning off all the lights long after the employees have left. The stories go on and on. The rich do not live the lifestyle of the rich—they stay rich because they are frugal misers at heart.

9 Assess your income and what you can do with it. 80% of modern millionaires were able to get there on annual incomes of $55,000 or less. Even meager savings eventually add up to thousands or millions of dollars.

10 When you look at a job, always know how much the head honcho gets paid because this will later affect your income in terms of promotion, benefits and future potential earnings. If you are gunning for a six figure salary and the current CEO is getting by on $300,000 a year, then maybe the job is not for you.

11 Find alternative ways to generate income if you are unhappy about your current level of earnings or the amount of the salary you currently have. This can mean looking for other employment with better pay or benefits or finding ways to boost your income little by little. This can mean starting a cottage industry business, learning to invest, buying and selling online or any number of means to add to your nest egg.

12 Create forms of passive income, the type of income that you receive with little to no effort. Examples of this include: rent from property you own, licensing patents or dividends and returns from investments.

Passive income can come from many sources. Exploiting the business possibilities of the Internet through blogs or sales from eBay or Amazon is one way to add to your income with minimal effort. The truly wealthy prefer passive income anytime. It frees up time for you to do what you want, even while you earn.

13 Be diverse. Create streams of income, do not rely on one large river. A job that pays $3M is great, but an accident or sudden layoff can cut you off. Think outside your salary. A job paying you $1M a year, plus real estate profits that amount to $1M and another $1M from stock is a far easier and safer thing to manage.

14 Learn to hold off gratification. A wealthy person knows how to delay gratification and sacrifice *the now* for later. This often comes with a positive attitude towards work and wealth, such as: “If I invest now, I will make 10% more later.”

The wealthy do not think of now, they think of the future. The present is merely an opportunity.

15 Change your mentality about spending. Do you really have to have that (place object here) *now?* The truly rich hold off gratification, knowing that what is trendy, popular or a must have today may not last until tomorrow.

16 Never be frightened of failure.

17 Be realistic. Growth and wealth do not appear overnight, unless you are lucky enough to win the lottery or find long lost treasure. Investments need time to mature and savings need time to accumulate. Patience will be well rewarded. The wealthy know that scrimping now will lead to better results in the future.

18 Create a sense of urgency in your life. Do not wait for things to *happen to you.* You may think that you are playing safe by waiting around or looking for the next big deal. This is the financial equivalent sitting around. Take risks, invest, start the business *now.* Seize opportunities the moment they happen. The first to get there often wins, leaving the losers in the dust.

Taking stock of what you have right now can have some advantageous surprises. For one, you may find out that you have more than you think. Second, it gives you a clear cut place to start and helps you find balance as well as set goals. After all, you cannot move forward without knowing where you come from.

Cutting Corners Where They Matter

When it comes to wealth generation, another important factor that is hard to follow is "living within your means." For many people, living in debt has become the norm. It is common for the average person to be buried in debt before they reach the age of 25. A consumer-driven economy based on floating credit also creates the impression that wealth means more products. After taking a hard look at your assets and income, now you have to check your lifestyle and see where you can cut down on expenses.

19 Write down your expenses. Do not lie to yourself. There is nothing like seeing it in black and white (or red). Keep track of your expenses on a spreadsheet or if you prefer, in a notebook. It gives you a concrete idea of where you are spending too much and where you are spending too little.

If you are looking to save more, write down everything you buy and keep track of it. Do you really need to spend $5 a day on designer coffee? That amounts to $1800 dollars a year just on your morning cup of Joe. Is it paramount to have the latest car every single year when you are hip deep in auto loans?

20 Cut those credit cards. The average person owns at least seven cards. The average number you need to sustain a good to great credit score? The answer is one or two. One well-managed card does more for your credit score than the dozen overextended cards you have. If you can manage without one, why not cut them all? Your credit score is not just affected by cards, but by other loans you have in your name, like your mortgage or auto loan.

21 Ruthlessly cut out all the services you do not need and monitor those you do. One millionaire famously counted the sheets in toilet paper rolls because he thought suppliers were overcharging him. He was right.

22 Before you cut those cards however, understand the utilization ratio: the total credit used versus the total credit available to you. Many people keep multiple cards for fear that one or more lines will be cut, increasing the ratio over time. The goal is to have a very low ratio compared to debt, low balances and even lower interest.

23 Get a free copy of your credit report. Dispute any outdated items. Keep in mind that items should slide off, not stay on. Focus on judgments, liens and any items that undermine your potential to lenders.

24 Understand how interest affects your debt. The wealthy understand how interest works for investments, for loans and how it compounds over time. Those who are not wealthy do not.

Compound interest is interest that is added to the principle at certain intervals on the debt. This means that the loan/balance of a certain loan gets higher over time and you end up paying more interest.

Compounding rates differ but can be legally done on a yearly, quarterly, yearly or even daily basis. A loan with a starting principal of $1000 charged with 20% interest per year turns into $1200 at the end of the first year and so on. In contrast, simple interest does not add to the principal of the loan, but is the amount charged for use of that money or loan.

25 PAY DEBT OFF ASAP. Pay more than the minimum on loans. Satisfy the interest and part of the principal—the debt amount will lessen over time and the bonus is you pay it off faster. The more you pay now, the less you pay later.

26 Keep records of any and all transactions over the Internet or phone, especially if you are fixing your finances.

a. Print or save any changes to your account.
b. When calling customer service, ask for the representative's employee number and record the time of the call in the event you need to follow up on a request.
c. Keep exact files and amounts.
d. Keep copies of everything.

27 Be hyper-vigilant when it comes to cards, loans or mortgages. Look for ways to lower interest, increase payments and keep an eye out for changes that could affect your loans.

28 Make a budget and stick to it. Think of it as a budge-it. Once you make it, you do not budge-it. Monthly and weekly budgets should be calculated to the penny.

29 The truly wealthy or those who want to be consider debt to be death to their portfolio. They only allow themselves to go into debt when they need it, and in that case they often refer to it as capital or even better, they often get it from someone else.

Keep the motto in mind when working with debt and get rid of it as soon as possible.

30 Separate your accounts to keep track of your money. Keep a savings account, an investment account and an earnings account.

31 Know the consequences of forbearing or deferring loans. The breathing room you get is often paid back threefold in capitalized interest or an increased loan principal.

32 Create an emergency fund or funds. These accounts should contain the equivalent of 3 to 6 months salary using low risk accounts

(savings, certificates of deposits or insured money market accounts) as a safety net not just for your finances but for unexpected events in your life. This prevents you from dipping into your earnings or cashing in other income resources when unexpected and unwanted events happen, such as sudden illness.

33 Remember that you can grow rich now on money that you are throwing away. To be truly wealthy, you have to know that a simple dollar is an investment goldmine.

34 On average, millionaires spend more time selecting what to buy than buying the product itself. Why? Because they look for the best bargain before laying their money down—and ask for discounts before making a selection. Apply this principal to your life and watch your expenses go down.

Instead of selecting the first brand-name product you see, take the time to check what exactly you are getting. For example, many commercially branded cereal and grain products have exactly the same nutritional content as their generic cousins, at almost twice the price. Remember that you are paying more for the brand than you are for the product itself.

Millionaires and the wealthy also know the value of patience. Many stay in the first home they bought long after they can afford a more expensive one.

35 Never accept a deal at face value. Negotiate until you feel the terms are in your favor.

The most important thing you should know is that without financial freedom, you cannot be truly wealthy. The most important thing is to create a base: a lower debt to income ratio and leeway to save and put money aside for investing later on.

It also frees up your mind so you can implement the law of attraction. Implementing positive thinking in your life can draw in positive forces and create more and more goodwill and luck. It is hard to think positive when you are constantly worrying about bills or making payments. By thinking positive and creating more positivity in your life, you bring in not just monetary wealth but a wealth in your personal life as well.

Investing and Managing Your Wealth: Becoming Truly Wealthy

Once you have established a firm financial foundation or put aside a little money, it is time to learn to invest. Many first time investors fall into the trap of waiting, and waiting until they "have enough." The first thing you have to do is nix that notion, right now. You will find out by reading the tips that even measly amounts can add up to great amounts over time.

Others balk at investing because they think "I do not know enough to be a player." That is right. You do not. The truly wealthy understand how money works and never start sentences with the words "I do not know." If you do not understand investing and how it works, it is time to start to do the legwork.

Investing 101

The primary focus of investing is making your money work for you instead of working for your money. Many wealthy people have perfected the art of creating their wealth instead of giving a service. Building wealth also means creating wealth that is sustainable and continues to generate even in the event that you are unable to work.

36 Learn the difference between having a high income and being truly wealthy. High incomes do not necessarily mean that you are rich, especially if this income comes from only one source.

The myth persists that you can only be truly wealthy if you come into family money or are born into a home of silver spoons, silk sheets and antique furniture. Continue to believe in this myth, and you still have the mindset of the poor.

Many of the middle class believe that a high income job is the end all of their existence and work their butts off to get to a position that pays in five or six digits but end up baffled at how little they have by the time retirement rolls around.

For example, the average high level manager earns $200,000 a year, with benefits but stands to lose that income in the event of layoffs or illness. Although his income earning potential is high, it only comes from one source.

Contrast that with a middle level manager earning $50,000 a year. This middle manager, however, rents out properties in the city for another $500,000 and reaps dividends from stocks and bonds for another $100,000 a year. In the event of illness, death or mass layoffs, half of his earning potential is still secure.

The source of the latter's income is also easily passed on to future generations, securing wealth for the middle level manager's family.

37 Choose your investment goals as these will decide your allocation strategy later on. A broker or brokerage firm can help you decide on what your plans are, as well as help you begin investing.

38 Research the different types of investments as well as how risky they are. In general:

- Stocks – you purchase partial ownership of a company and as part-owner, are entitled to annual profits. However, many people buy stock to sell when the price is high, not for dividends. The practice of buying low and selling high is relatively low risk but the potential for reward is governed by market and highly emotional changes. Yes, stock is considered an emotional asset.

- Bonds – bonds are small loans to companies or governments that the investor pays for. They usually have fixed interest rates and are considered very safe and low risk investments. T-bills, municipal bonds and corporate bonds are some examples.

- Mutual fund – this involves pooling money together with other like-minded investors to buy a full portfolio, usually run by firms or money managers. This type of investment is often the starting point for many first-time investors, simply because it provides a more diverse portfolio from the get-go.

- REITS – these are companies that deal primarily with the ownership of real estate and manage a portfolio for you. They have the advantage of being diverse and easy to sell—as well as reduce the headache of managing your own property.

- Other alternatives – Generally these are the high-risk and high reward securities where the payoff can be huge but the risk is high. Real estate, commodities, FOREX, options and futures fall under this category.

39 Create an allocation strategy for your savings or income to minimize risk and spread out your investments to guarantee several streams of income versus just one.

Learn about investing and accounting before you start spreading the money around. Consult with brokers or brokerage firm, especially if you have a lot to invest. Take night courses or read investment books to understand what you are getting into.

40 For example, you have $100,000 dollars to invest. 35% ($35,000) could go to property or real estate, another 30% for stocks, 10% for venture capital, etc. An allocation strategy helps you maximize your investments and also gives you the ability to indulge in some high-risk behavior, if you so wish, without losing all your capital. The financial equivalent of putting all your eggs in one basket, such as investing in all one type of equity, is portfolio suicide.

41 Support the traditional and explore the new. Opportunities grow with the growth of the Internet and the advent of technology. The Internet is not just a place to go to. The exponential growth of business and the changing face of technology creates more and more investment opportunities for the modern investor, as well as the modern entrepreneur.

42 Account for every cent, every nickel, every dime and quarter. The saying goes you never know the value of money until you have to dig around the couch cushions for it. The truly wealthy know that every penny can be put to good use. Money is stagnant only when you want it to be, or when it flies out of your hands.

43 Even small amounts matter. Many people say they will invest only when they have x amount, but even a small investment of $1000 can give you great returns in the future. By thinking of returns instead of instant cash or how much you have on hand, you create your wealth through possibilities.

Saving 10,000 a year with a 10% rate of return and seeding that account with an additional 10,000 per year will yield $128,000+ after 10 years. If you start with $5,000, you end up with about $94,000 after said 10 years. That doesn't count the interest the account would generate for years after.

44 Invest your money as early as you can. The true friend of money is always time and the passage of it. The longer money sits and the more interest it collects, the higher the chances that you will reap thousands of dollars in returns.

A great example for this is the 401(k). Many Americans simply cannot wait until retirement and cash it in as soon as they can. But for what? A faster car, a bigger house or in some cases, that giant flat screen TV everyone else has.

Your 401(k) alone is a savings plan you must NEVER touch. Do the math. If you have an annual salary of $100,000 and contribute 10%, with a 50% employer match rate and no salary increases, you end up with $ 741,184.02 in 20 years. Increase the contribution to 12%, with all other factors constant and the amount rises to $889,420.89. Increase the time frame to 30 years and you end up with $2 *million.*

45 Buy stock, not product. If you love the product, chances are others will to. So why waste time buying the product when you can make money off the stock. This creates a) passive income and b) a higher chance of return on investments.

Take Apple. Apple's stock has risen over 12 times in the past five years, quadrupling dividends for investors. How many iPhones or iPods have you bought over the past five years? How much money do you think an average shareholder has made from the products you have been buying? Even with the death of its founder, Steve Jobs, Apple's stock remained strong and rose. Traditionally company stock falls with the death of visible CEOs or front men, but this was not true in this case.

One exception: keep in mind that sales do not make the stock. Activision is a company that markets and makes one of the biggest selling video games in the world, with sales totaling over 400,000 on the *first day* of the new installment release. However, their stock and shares have remained static for around 4 years.

46 Create assets that will make money for you with a minimum of effort. For example, investing in a restaurant does not require you to show up daily to manage the day-to-day running of the business, only to pay the management firm or keep the standard of a franchise.

47 Think long term. The truly wealthy do not count on single projects that net huge paychecks, but invest in opportunities that create

returns and dividends that last for years. Long term also means the ability of securities to mature. Thinking long term means having the ability to see the future in a sense—and finding projects that affect and create these futures.

48 Do not wait for business opportunities, create them. Entrepreneurs look at an empty lot and see possibility and a method for them to get rich. Those with a poor mindset simply see an empty lot. The rich look at garbage and see a garbage hauling business, a rust-cleaning service, a recycling center. Those with a poor mindset see only the discarded tires, the dirt and the weeds.

49 Another great secret is to never care where you money comes from. Many people balk at investing in businesses that are not "sexy" perhaps because they do not want to tell people at parties that they got rich off sewage.

Truly wealthy people spread their money around and reap them in regardless if they were earned because of sewage or flowers. Who cares if it comes up in cocktail conversation?

50 Always think in terms of specific assets versus their overall value in the market. The truly wealthy do not rely on the ups and downs of the market, but the possible opportunities that stem from them.

For example, the real estate market may be down during the recession but right now savvy investors are buying up foreclosed property in great locations for half prices for later investment.

51 Know when to hold off, reassess and quit. Investors will say no. But not all of them will. Those with a poor mindset go to the bank for a loan, get rejected and never think about their idea or opportunity again. The wealthy mindset goes to the bank for a loan, gets rejected, redrafts the proposal and returns to get the approval.

The poor mindset goes into business not knowing the risks of the deal and is baffled when the fallout occurs. The wealthy mindset goes into a deal, knows the risk and gets out if things are going bad. Always follow your gut and do your research. Know when to back off from risky or unethical deals will not only take your money but have effects of your freedom.

52 Accept that there will be instances where you will experience some loss, such as when stock goes down or remains stagnant, therefore not providing you with the expected dividends. Accept that this will change as well.

53 Do not join the bandwagon: just because everyone is putting their money in it, does not mean you should. Get rich quick schemes are simply schemes.

54 Forget compartmentalizing your money. Every penny is important so do not think of it as a bonus or extra pay. The wealthy put every single cent to good use and are able to account for all of them.

The lesson here is to value every single dollar you earn. One millionaire started by investing $25, that is right, $25 in a mutual fund. He could not afford any more at the time, since he worked a menial job. As his pool grew, so did the amount of his investments. He is now worth multi-millions.

55 Learn about taxes and how to use them to your advantage, not the other way around.

56 The truly wealthy know how to make taxes work for them. Never be afraid to learn and ask. Instead of having someone do it for you, learn how to do it yourself.

57 Finally, never invest if you are not willing to wait. Otherwise, you are throwing your money away like a gambling addict at a poker table.

The truly wealth think of investing as a game that pays out and is a fun to play. Never for once think that they got there by simple luck. It takes a lot of research, studying and waiting to get there. The poor make excuses and say, they never have enough time between their jobs, their family and whatever other obligations they have.

The wealthy create the time to invest and invest in their time as well.

However, the main difference is this: they enjoy it. They enjoy the time they spend reading investment books. They enjoy reading the reports, watching the stock market and simply *love the game of money.* This is an attitude you need to become successful when you move to invest. This is the attitude that makes winners and makes the wealthy.

Making and Protecting Your Money

The average millionaire or comfortably wealthy person works for himself or owns a business. This is a law that is hard to follow. Most people think a business is a risky proposition simply because there are so many factors that affect the success of a business. A million things can go wrong, but a million things can also go right.

The wealth mindset is one that works for itself, cashing in on your own ideas and labor. The poor mindset works for others, laboring for a minimum cut of the profit.

The idea of working for yourself can be scary. Many first-time business owners fail because they sink everything they have into one venture and never recommit when the road to success gets rocky. The wealthy and the rich stick with their business plan and move forward regardless of the events, confident in their success.

58 Do something that you love, because you will never feel like it is work. The success stories of many entrepreneurs and millionaires always begin with this line "I love...[insert hobby, passion or interest here] so I…."

Money always follows passion and the upside is, you will never feel like you worked a day in your life. Ask yourself what you love to do, what you are good at and how important it is to you. Once you know what it is, you will know what venture to begin.

59 Alternatively, find a need for something you love and fill it. Filling a need or creating a need is an excellent starting point for a business. Curves Gym combined the owner's need for fitness and hatred of being ogled while at the gym.

She provided a women's only gym *without* mirrors, filling a need many women did not even know existed. Women lined up around the street to work out at this gym and it boasts hundreds of franchises around the US today.

60 Do not be afraid to do something humble—many a business has expanded from humble origins and cottage industries. No idea is too small, no business is "stupid".

61 Make sure your business fits your lifestyle. If you hate nightclubs, why start one? Why start a golfing business when you have never picked up a club in your life and have no interest in doing so?

62 Those who cannot run a business, invest in one. It takes the headache out of the management and gives you profit without the effort.

63 The wealthy know when to expand their business. Those who want to be truly rich run multiple businesses. Take Nigella Lawson, who started with a cooking show and now has a line of products and even utensils. One business, different umbrellas. Different umbrellas, one profit.

64 The business should never be static, but it should be familiar. Take a cue from top restaurants. They constantly change or update their menus but keep the customer favorites around.

65 Be the best. There are *no* exceptions to this rule. Provide the best service, the fastest delivery, the highest quality, the newest products. Follow these rules and the customers will come.

A sub rule to this secret is to always strive to continue to be the best. Once you have set a standard, customers and clients will expect you to maintain it. Many a business has experienced fallout after reaching heights due to declining service or worsening product. Take a cue from timeless products and services that continue to make money over the years. They never balk or shirk when it comes to quality. Even if it means making their customers pay a little extra.

66 Your business is defined by its employees—especially if you decide to go into any type of service industry. Hire for attitude, train for skill.

Never keep an employee who is not worth the salary you pay. Never tolerate stupidity, slowness or excuses. Instead, screen, evaluate and expect change. Millionaires never take slack from their employees. They never hesitate when the time comes to let one go.

67 Learn to recommit. Every business owner experiences fall out, bad sales or some sort of failure. There will always be a time when you fall into the red. It takes perseverance to go back into the black.

68 Economize where it counts. Find the best deals for raw product to maximize profit.

69 The truly wealthy know how to make profit with minimal expenditure. Reduce overhead, especially when it comes to trappings. A huge corner office with the antique desk and leather seats will not mean much when you are scrambling to pay the bills.

Protecting Your Money

Once you have money, you will take time to protect it by avoiding future catastrophes. Be cautious and always assume the worst. Do not go through life thinking that other people will not take advantage of you or that your money is not important to them. A careless mistake can cost you a fortune. A careless demeanor opens you up to attack. And you will never know where it is going to come from.

Now that you have the money, you have to take the steps to protect it from unscrupulous beings. Many a millionaire's downfall came from lawsuits from hungry money-grubbing relatives or the greed from immediate family. The media is packed with celebrity stories where the 'evil' spouse gets millions in the divorce, millions they never earned simply because the high earner took no precautions.

In the case of lawsuits, anything personal amounts to what you or your companies are worth. Lawyers love public information and can easily figure out what you are worth by accessing public records. Transferring the bulk of your wealth to foundations, trusts or corporations ensures that these stay well out of the public's eye or are untouchable in the event you are attacked.

Protecting your money now ensures that it will continue to benefit you and your family for years and decades to come.

70 Millionaires and the truly wealthy never put assets in their name and guard their personal assets zealously. They use corporations and protect themselves with liability insurance. Corporate entities are used to operate businesses, partnerships are made with the idea that if all goes to hell, it is time to get out. Use trusts, family partnerships and protect your personal assets and wealth.

71 Turn yourself into a stealthy, moving target. Never be conspicuous about your wealth and forego the trappings of it. Remember: the bigger, flashier bird is always easier to bring down. The birds that fly low, fly below the radar and detection.

72 Begin asset protection early to prevent any mishaps. Never let yourself get caught in the trap of beginning asset protection when you are already in heaps of trouble!

There is nothing like being prepared. Besides, transferring assets when you are being sued is illegal and can land you in jail (plus you lose everything). Protect your personal assets from claims and unscrupulous parties!

73 Create a clear-cut and legal will, even if you are only 32 years old. Make sure you know where your money is going. Many people put off the idea of the will simply because it makes them face their own mortality which is always wrong.

Update and notarize yearly, or anytime you like. A will prevents many a family feud, protects your interests long after you are gone and ensures that money that you share keeps going where you want it go. Without a will, chaos will ensue, especially if your personal fortune and business assets are worth six digits or more.

For businesses, the equivalent of a will is known as succession planning. Many successful business have failed because an epic predecessor was not able to carefully plan who would succeed him in the event of his death.

Follow the example of Steve Jobs and create a succession plan for your business *before you even get sick or retire.* Many family corporations create a version of this by grooming successors from within the family and stipulating conditions to be met in order to inherit or run the business.

74 Never enter any partnership, including conjugal ones, without a back-up plan or a clear way out. That is what prenuptial agreements are for. Do not let a future ex-spouse pull a Paul McCartney on you.

75 Never put all your money into one humungous deal. Diversity is the key to true wealth. Keep in mind that those eggs in one basket are more liable to break if the basket is too heavy.

76 Once you become wealthy, do not forget the rules and secrets that got you there. First time millionaires and lotto winners often blow through their millions by acquiring status symbols like mad and often end up with nothing. Continue to extol the virtues that got you to where you are now. Live simply and below your means, even if you are worth enough to make it to the Forbes 500 list.

77 The final timeless wealth secret. Money is meant to shared, not hoarded. Follow the Rockefeller rule: 10% of your worth is meant to shared. This creates more for you.

Conclusion

There is no shortcut to instant wealth. Being rich means playing a game that lasts for years. The truly wealthy not only look forward to this game, but also look forward to playing it. By following these timeless secrets, you learn the value of hard work, patience and reap the rewards for years to come.

Never be complacent and put off your wealth creation for tomorrow. True wealth and real wealth starts by making these changes today. Break that piggy bank and start investing *now.*

Wealth creation is both a complex strategy and a waiting game but by following these 77 tips, you can be on your way to true wealth, a comfortable lifestyle and living your life financially free.

www.ingramcontent.com/pod-product-compliance
Ingram Content Group UK Ltd.
Pitfield, Milton Keynes, MK11 3LW, UK
UKHW051133260726
13967UKWH00010B/3024

9 781312 863552